The Cute Cookie

by Liza Charlesworth

The Cute Cookie

by Liza Charlesworth

ISBN: 978-1-338-18892-9

Magic Fairy

by Liza Charlesworth

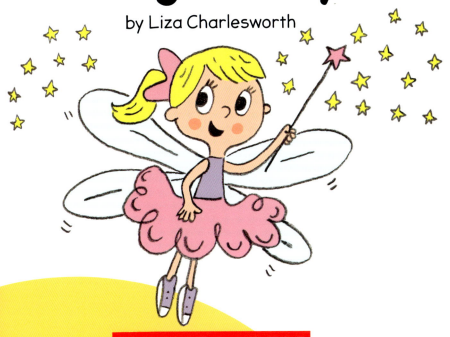

SCHOLASTIC

Magic Fairy

by Liza Charlesworth

No part of this publication may be reproduced, stored in a retrieval system, or transmitted in any form or by any means, electronic, mechanical, photocopying, recording, or otherwise, without written permission of the publisher. For information regarding permission, write to Scholastic Inc., Attention: Permissions Department, 557 Broadway, New York, NY 10012.

ISBN: 978-1-338-18893-6
Illustrated by Eric Barclay
Art Director: Tannaz Fassihi; Designer: Michelle H. Kim

Copyright © 2017 by Liza Charlesworth. All rights reserved. Published by Scholastic Inc.

11 10   68   22 23/0

Printed in China. First printing, June 2017.

www.scholastic.com

ISBN: 978-1-338-18893-6

Too Sweet

by Liza Charlesworth

Too Sweet

by Liza Charlesworth

No part of this publication may be reproduced, stored in a retrieval system, or transmitted in any form or by any means, electronic, mechanical, photocopying, recording, or otherwise, without written permission of the publisher. For information regarding permission, write to Scholastic Inc., Attention: Permissions Department, 557 Broadway, New York, NY 10012.

ISBN: 978-1-338-18894-3
Illustrated by Eric Barclay
Art Director: Tannaz Fassihi; Designer: Michelle H. Kim

Copyright © 2017 by Liza Charlesworth. All rights reserved. Published by Scholastic Inc.

11 10   68   22 23/0

Printed in China. First printing, June 2017.

www.scholastic.com

ISBN: 978-1-338-18894-3

The Human Beans

by Liza Charlesworth

The Human Beans

by Liza Charlesworth

No part of this publication may be reproduced, stored in a retrieval system, or transmitted in any form or by any means, electronic, mechanical, photocopying, recording, or otherwise, without written permission of the publisher. For information regarding permission, write to Scholastic Inc., Attention: Permissions Department, 557 Broadway, New York, NY 10012.

ISBN: 978-1-338-18895-0
Illustrated by Eric Barclay
Art Director: Tannaz Fassihi; Designer: Michelle H. Kim

Copyright © 2017 by Liza Charlesworth. All rights reserved. Published by Scholastic Inc.

11 10   68   22 23/0

Printed in China. First printing, June 2017.

www.scholastic.com

ISBN: 978-1-338-18895-0

I Am Just Too Small

by Liza Charlesworth

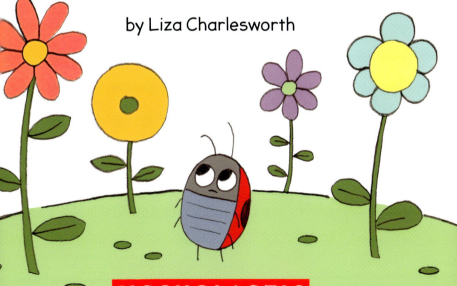

I Am Just Too Small

by Liza Charlesworth

No part of this publication may be reproduced, stored in a retrieval system, or transmitted in any form or by any means, electronic, mechanical, photocopying, recording, or otherwise, without written permission of the publisher. For information regarding permission, write to Scholastic Inc., Attention: Permissions Department, 557 Broadway, New York, NY 10012.

ISBN: 978-1-338-18896-7
Illustrated by Eric Barclay
Art Director: Tannaz Fassihi; Designer: Michelle H. Kim

Copyright © 2017 by Liza Charlesworth. All rights reserved. Published by Scholastic Inc.

11 10 68 22 23/0

Printed in China. First printing, June 2017.

ISBN: 978-1-338-18896-7

The Ice Cream Cone

by Liza Charlesworth

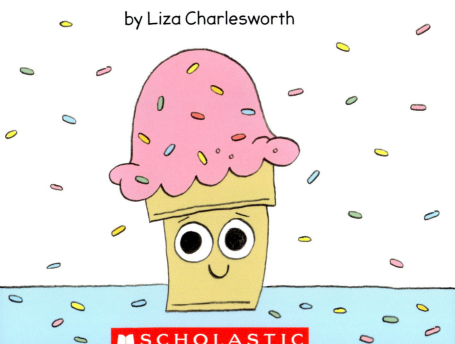

The Ice Cream Cone

by Liza Charlesworth

No part of this publication may be reproduced, stored in a retrieval system, or transmitted in any form or by any means, electronic, mechanical, photocopying, recording, or otherwise, without written permission of the publisher. For information regarding permission, write to Scholastic Inc., Attention: Permissions Department, 557 Broadway, New York, NY 10012.

ISBN: 978-1-338-18897-4
Illustrated by Eric Barclay
Art Director: Tannaz Fassihi; Designer: Michelle H. Kim

Copyright © 2017 by Liza Charlesworth. All rights reserved. Published by Scholastic Inc.

11 10 68 22 23/0

Printed in China. First printing, June 2017.

www.scholastic.com

ISBN: 978-1-338-18897-4

Surprise!

by Liza Charlesworth

Surprise!

by Liza Charlesworth

No part of this publication may be reproduced, stored in a retrieval system, or transmitted in any form or by any means, electronic, mechanical, photocopying, recording, or otherwise, without written permission of the publisher. For information regarding permission, write to Scholastic Inc., Attention: Permissions Department, 557 Broadway, New York, NY 10012.

ISBN: 978-1-338-18898-1
Illustrated by Eric Barclay
Art Director: Tannaz Fassihi; Designer: Michelle H. Kim

Copyright © 2017 by Liza Charlesworth. All rights reserved. Published by Scholastic Inc.

11 10   68   22 23/0

Printed in China. First printing, June 2017.

www.scholastic.com

ISBN: 978-1-338-18898-1

My Pet Spot

by Liza Charlesworth

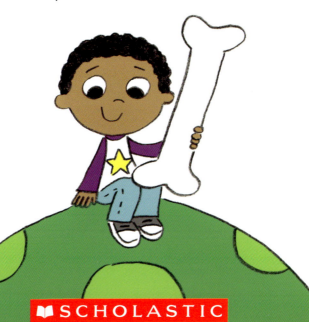

My Pet Spot

by Liza Charlesworth

No part of this publication may be reproduced, stored in a retrieval system, or transmitted in any form or by any means, electronic, mechanical, photocopying, recording, or otherwise, without written permission of the publisher. For information regarding permission, write to Scholastic Inc., Attention: Permissions Department, 557 Broadway, New York, NY 10012.

ISBN: 978-1-338-18899-8
Illustrated by Eric Barclay
Art Director: Tannaz Fassihi; Designer: Michelle H. Kim

Copyright © 2017 by Liza Charlesworth. All rights reserved. Published by Scholastic Inc.

11 10   68   22 23/0

Printed in China. First printing, June 2017.

www.scholastic.com

ISBN: 978-1-338-18899-8

A Polite Pirate

by Liza Charlesworth

A Polite Pirate

by Liza Charlesworth

No part of this publication may be reproduced, stored in a retrieval system, or transmitted in any form or by any means, electronic, mechanical, photocopying, recording, or otherwise, without written permission of the publisher. For information regarding permission, write to Scholastic Inc., Attention: Permissions Department, 557 Broadway, New York, NY 10012.

ISBN: 978-1-338-18900-1
Illustrated by Eric Barclay
Art Director: Tannaz Fassihi; Designer: Michelle H. Kim

Copyright © 2017 by Liza Charlesworth. All rights reserved. Published by Scholastic Inc.

11 10   68   22 23/0

Printed in China. First printing, June 2017.

www.scholastic.com

ISBN: 978-1-338-18900-1

I Am Not Afraid

by Liza Charlesworth

I Am Not Afraid

by Liza Charlesworth

No part of this publication may be reproduced, stored in a retrieval system, or transmitted in any form or by any means, electronic, mechanical, photocopying, recording, or otherwise, without written permission of the publisher. For information regarding permission, write to Scholastic Inc., Attention: Permissions Department, 557 Broadway, New York, NY 10012.

ISBN: 978-1-338-18901-8
Illustrated by Eric Barclay
Art Director: Tannaz Fassihi; Designer: Michelle H. Kim

Copyright © 2017 by Liza Charlesworth. All rights reserved. Published by Scholastic Inc.

11 10   68   22 23/0

Printed in China. First printing, June 2017.

www.scholastic.com

ISBN: 978-1-338-18901-8

Where Is Bob?

by Liza Charlesworth

Where Is Bob?

by Liza Charlesworth

No part of this publication may be reproduced, stored in a retrieval system, or transmitted in any form or by any means, electronic, mechanical, photocopying, recording, or otherwise, without written permission of the publisher. For information regarding permission, write to Scholastic Inc., Attention: Permissions Department, 557 Broadway, New York, NY 10012.

ISBN: 978-1-338-18902-5
Illustrated by Catherine L. Drolet
Art Director: Tannaz Fassihi; Designer: Michelle H. Kim

Copyright © 2017 by Liza Charlesworth. All rights reserved. Published by Scholastic Inc.

11 10   68   22 23/0

Printed in China. First printing, June 2017.

www.scholastic.com

ISBN: 978-1-338-18902-5

Little Red Pen

by Liza Charlesworth

Little Red Pen

by Liza Charlesworth

No part of this publication may be reproduced, stored in a retrieval system, or transmitted in any form or by any means, electronic, mechanical, photocopying, recording, or otherwise, without written permission of the publisher. For information regarding permission, write to Scholastic Inc., Attention: Permissions Department, 557 Broadway, New York, NY 10012.

ISBN: 978-1-338-18903-2
Illustrated by Catherine L. Drolet
Art Director: Tannaz Fassihi; Designer: Michelle H. Kim

Copyright © 2017 by Liza Charlesworth. All rights reserved. Published by Scholastic Inc.

11 10   6 8   22 23/0

Printed in China. First printing, June 2017.

www.scholastic.com

ISBN: 978-1-338-18903-

The Giant

by Liza Charlesworth

The Giant

by Liza Charlesworth

No part of this publication may be reproduced, stored in a retrieval system, or transmitted in any form or by any means, electronic, mechanical, photocopying, recording, or otherwise, without written permission of the publisher. For information regarding permission, write to Scholastic Inc., Attention: Permissions Department, 557 Broadway, New York, NY 10012.

ISBN: 978-1-338-18904-9
Illustrated by Catherine L. Drolet
Art Director: Tannaz Fassihi; Designer: Michelle H. Kim

Copyright © 2017 by Liza Charlesworth. All rights reserved. Published by Scholastic Inc.

11 10   68   22 23/0

Printed in China. First printing, June 2017.

ISBN: 978-1-338-18904-9

The Best Balloon

by Liza Charlesworth

SCHOLASTIC

The Best Balloon

by Liza Charlesworth

No part of this publication may be reproduced, stored in a retrieval system, or transmitted in any form or by any means, electronic, mechanical, photocopying, recording, or otherwise, without written permission of the publisher. For information regarding permission, write to Scholastic Inc., Attention: Permissions Department, 557 Broadway, New York, NY 10012.
ISBN: 978-1-338-18905-6
Illustrated by Catherine L. Drolet
Art Director: Tannaz Fassihi; Designer: Michelle H. Kim
Copyright © 2017 by Liza Charlesworth. All rights reserved. Published by Scholastic Inc.
11 10   68   22 23/0
Printed in China. First printing, June 2017.

ISBN: 978-1-338-18905-6

Monster Soup

by Liza Charlesworth

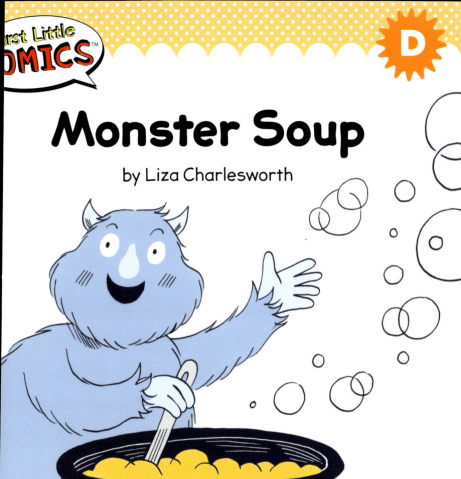

Monster Soup

by Liza Charlesworth

No part of this publication may be reproduced, stored in a retrieval system, or transmitted in any form or by any means, electronic, mechanical, photocopying, recording, or otherwise, without written permission of the publisher. For information regarding permission, write to Scholastic Inc., Attention: Permissions Department, 557 Broadway, New York, NY 10012.

ISBN: 978-1-338-18906-3
Illustrated by Catherine L. Drolet
Art Director: Tannaz Fassihi; Designer: Michelle H. Kim

Copyright © 2017 by Liza Charlesworth. All rights reserved. Published by Scholastic Inc.

11 10   68   22 23/0

Printed in China. First printing, June 2017.

www.scholastic.com

ISBN: 978-1-338-18906-3

The Couch Potato

by Liza Charlesworth

The Couch Potato

by Liza Charlesworth

No part of this publication may be reproduced, stored in a retrieval system, or transmitted in any form or by any means, electronic, mechanical, photocopying, recording, or otherwise, without written permission of the publisher. For information regarding permission, write to Scholastic Inc., Attention: Permissions Department, 557 Broadway, New York, NY 10012.

ISBN: 978-1-338-18907-0
Illustrated by Catherine L. Drolet
Art Director: Tannaz Fassihi; Designer: Michelle H. Kim

Copyright © 2017 by Liza Charlesworth. All rights reserved. Published by Scholastic Inc.

11 10   68   22 23/0

Printed in China. First printing, June 2017.

www.scholastic.com

ISBN: 978-1-338-18907-0

Sue's Shoes

by Liza Charlesworth

Sue's Shoes

by Liza Charlesworth

No part of this publication may be reproduced, stored in a retrieval system, or transmitted in any form or by any means, electronic, mechanical, photocopying, recording, or otherwise, without written permission of the publisher. For information regarding permission, write to Scholastic Inc., Attention: Permissions Department, 557 Broadway, New York, NY 10012.

ISBN: 978-1-338-18908-7
Illustrated by Catherine L. Drolet
Art Director: Tannaz Fassihi; Designer: Michelle H. Kim
Copyright © 2017 by Liza Charlesworth. All rights reserved. Published by Scholastic Inc.

11 10   68   22 23/0

Printed in China. First printing, June 2017.

ISBN: 978-1-338-18908-

Pam and Sam

by Liza Charlesworth

Pam and Sam

by Liza Charlesworth

No part of this publication may be reproduced, stored in a retrieval system, or transmitted in any form or by any means, electronic, mechanical, photocopying, recording, or otherwise, without written permission of the publisher. For information regarding permission, write to Scholastic Inc., Attention: Permissions Department, 557 Broadway, New York, NY 10012.

ISBN: 978-1-338-18909-4
Illustrated by Catherine L. Drolet
Art Director: Tannaz Fassihi; Designer: Michelle H. Kim

Copyright © 2017 by Liza Charlesworth. All rights reserved. Published by Scholastic Inc.

11 10   68   22 23/0

Printed in China. First printing, June 2017.

www.scholastic.com

ISBN: 978-1-338-18909-4

Grumpy Troll

by Liza Charlesworth

Grumpy Troll

by Liza Charlesworth

No part of this publication may be reproduced, stored in a retrieval system, or transmitted in any form or by any means, electronic, mechanical, photocopying, recording, or otherwise, without written permission of the publisher. For information regarding permission, write to Scholastic Inc., Attention: Permissions Department, 557 Broadway, New York, NY 10012.

ISBN: 978-1-338-18910-0
Illustrated by Catherine L. Drolet
Art Director: Tannaz Fassihi; Designer: Michelle H. Kim

Copyright © 2017 by Liza Charlesworth. All rights reserved. Published by Scholastic Inc.

11 10   68   22 23/0

Printed in China. First printing, June 2017.

www.scholastic.com

ISBN: 978-1-338-18910-0

The Three Little Cats

by Liza Charlesworth

The Three Little Cats

by Liza Charlesworth

No part of this publication may be reproduced, stored in a retrieval system, or transmitted in any form or by any means, electronic, mechanical, photocopying, recording, or otherwise, without written permission of the publisher. For information regarding permission, write to Scholastic Inc., Attention: Permissions Department, 557 Broadway, New York, NY 10012.

ISBN: 978-1-338-18911-7
Illustrated by Catherine L. Drolet
Art Director: Tannaz Fassihi; Designer: Michelle H. Kim

Copyright © 2017 by Liza Charlesworth. All rights reserved. Published by Scholastic Inc.

11 10   68   22 23/0

Printed in China. First printing, June 2017.

www.scholastic.com

ISBN: 978-1-338-18911-7